Ask Dave

Dave Winfield answers kids' questions about baseball and life

PIONEER  BOOKS

Andrews and McMeel
A Universal Press Syndicate Company
Kansas City

Ask Dave: Dave Winfield answers kids' questions about baseball and life copyright © 1994 by *Saint Paul Pioneer Press*. All rights reserved. Printed in the United States of America. No part of this book may be used or reproduced in any manner whatsoever without the written permission of Andrews and McMeel and *Saint Paul Pioneer Press* except in the case of reprints in the context of a review. For information, write Andrews and McMeel, a Universal Press Syndicate Company, 4900 Main St., Kansas City, Missouri 64112.

Pioneer Books are published for *Saint Paul Pioneer Press* by Andrews and McMeel. Additional copies may be ordered by calling (800) 642-6480.

Library of Congress Cataloging-in Publication Data

Winfield, Dave, 1951–
    Ask Dave : Dave Winfield answers kids' questions about baseball and life.
    p. cm.
    ISBN 0-8362-8057-1 : $7.95
    1. Winfield, Dave, 1951– —Interviews—Juvenile literature. 2. Winfield, Dave, 1951– —Views on life—Juvenile literature. 3. Baseball players—United States—Interviews—Juvenile literature. 4. Children's questions and answers—Juvenile literature.
    [1. Baseball—Miscellanea. 2. Winfield, Dave, 1951- . 3. Questions and answers.]
    I. Title.
GV865.W57A3   1994
796.357'092—dc20
[B]
                                                                       94-225
                                                                         CIP
                                                                          AC

PIONEER BOOKS

Ask Dave Editor: Don Effenberger
Editorial Director: Ken Doctor
Promotion Director: Chris Oshikata
Design Director: Lauri Treston

Cover photo: Saint Paul Pioneer Press
Cover illustrations: Kirk Lyttle
Back cover photo: Gordy Jones

Acknowledgments: Mario Casciano, for assistance in gathering photos and background information; Dave St. Peter, for assistance in compiling career data.

Contents

A Message From Dave Winfield   5

Division 1: Talking Baseball   7
CHAPTER 1: My Pitch   8
CHAPTER 2: My Turn at Bat   22
CHAPTER 3: Inside Baseball   36
CHAPTER 4: Personal Milestones   48
CHAPTER 5: Life With the Twins   54

Division 2: My Life   61
CHAPTER 1: Childhood Memories   62
CHAPTER 2: Vital Stats   70
CHAPTER 3: The Spotlight's Glare   80
CHAPTER 4: Youth Efforts   86
CHAPTER 5: Keeping Fit   92

Division 3: Leading the Way   97
Career at a Glance   98
The Winfield Foundation   101
How to Order Winfield Books   103

BILL ALKOFER/**ST. PAUL PIONEER PRESS**

A MESSAGE FROM DAVE WINFIELD

One lesson I learned early on is that individual success, whether in athletics or in life, really takes a team effort. Talent by itself can carry an individual—no matter how gifted—only so far.

To develop the skills and to stay on course toward a goal, every one of us needs a behind-the-scenes team of true fans. We can count on these loyal supporters—parents, teachers, coaches and friends—to help us develop our special gifts and root us on even when the going gets tough.

I know that without the support of my mother, brother and extended family, my coaches and teachers, I probably wouldn't have found my true calling or been prepared to make the most of my natural talents when my chance came.

In sports and in life, a coach, as well as true fans, will never give up on a player or person. In return, each of us owes these special people a 100 percent effort every time. That means being prepared to do our best when it's our turn at bat, whether it's before cheering fans on the sports field or on our own in the classroom or on the job.

Likewise, we each have an obligation to return, in our own way, that show of support by sharing what we've learned and by offering a helping hand to others.

That's one big reason I began my nationally distributed Ask Dave newspaper column and why I created the Dave Winfield Foundation in 1977. It's my way of saying thanks to all the people who have been there for me over the years.

Also, let me say a few words about the importance of role models. I hope that I have been a role model for many of you, and I want you to remember that there will be many others who want to follow in your steps and be like you. So, make your choices wisely—and decide to be a good role model!

Best wishes to all,

D. Winfield

3,000! Dave acknowledges the Metrodome crowd's standing ovation after singling off Athletics pitcher Dennis Eckersley for his 3,000th hit.

JOHN DOMAN/**ST. PAUL PIONEER PRESS**

Chapter 1

DAVE DATA:
Dave is one of only five players with at least 3,000 hits and 450 home runs. The others are Hank Aaron, Willie Mays, Stan Musial and Carl Yastrzemski.

RICH MARSHALL/**ST. PAUL PIONEER PRESS**

SAFE AT HOME: Dave is all smiles during 1993 spring training after signing with his hometown team, the Minnesota Twins.

MY Pitch

 What advice can you give a 10-year-old boy on what it takes to get to the majors?
A.J., 10

Following that baseball dream

A I want you to know up front that many follow their dream of becoming a major-league baseball player, but only a few will make it. If you have natural talent and the desire and dedication—and if you receive first-class or professional instruction through clinics and camps—you may have a chance.

I advise you to play organized baseball as early as you can every year with the best talent you can find—from sandlot competition to high school and college. If you excel, a major-league scout will find you.

Heck, shoot for the stars! You may land on the moon and win a college baseball scholarship!

By pursuing your dream in baseball, you will travel a lot, make great friends and live a positive, healthy, wholesome way of life.

 What talents should I work on developing to become a professional baseball player?
Tray, 9

Emphasizing your strengths

Talking Baseball

A Well, all professional baseball players are able to either hit, run, field or throw pretty well. So, find out what your God-given ability is and where you excel. Work on that strength without neglecting the other areas. In time, you will find a position on the field that you are comfortable with. If you continue to improve and the scouts notice you, one day you may become that one in a million who becomes a professional baseball player.

Home run power

Q How do you hit so many home runs?
Steve

A To be a good hitter or a long-ball hitter, you must have one primary physical asset working for you—good hand-eye coordination. You must have it to make good, sufficient contact with the ball when it's pitched. So, if you want to be a good hitter, practice your hand and bat quickness and work on your overall strength to help you propel the ball great distances.

Coaches taught me to attack the ball and hit line drives. At this time in my life, my line drives sometimes carry a very long distance. A little suggestion: Go for the line drives. You'll get more hits, too.

The secrets of hitting

Q How do you manage to hit so well?
Justin, 12

Q Do you swing up or level when you hit, and do your arms get sore from the motion?
Michael

A My ability to hit comes from a combination of ingredients: good hand-eye coordination and good early coaching on how to attack the ball and hit it hard. Then, once I learned the techniques of hitting, I practiced correctly for many, many years.

My Pitch

RICH MARSHALL/**ST. PAUL PIONEER PRESS**

SLUGGING SECRETS: Demonstrating the finer points of batting, Dave shows some future sluggers the importance of a good follow-through.

Remember this when you're hitting: They say that seven out of 10 line drives are hits, whereas only one out of 10 fly balls falls in and only two to three out of 10 ground balls are hits. Simple math will tell you which approach will make you a better hitter.

The best angle to meet the pitched ball is slightly up, because the delivery from the pitcher's hand comes slightly down. So to make the best contact, you should swing slightly up.

Yes, my arms, legs and body do get sore from the activity, but that is part of the sacrifice in being good at anything like hitting a baseball.

Q I throw left-handed, and I'm a switch-hitter. I like to bat right-handed better, but should I keep working on my switch-hitting?

Andrew, 9

The value of switch-hitting

More switch-hitting benefits

A I've told many youngsters, parents and coaches over the years that if a person has the ability to hit well from both sides of the plate, he should do what he can to enhance those abilities. I guarantee that you'll become a more versatile and valuable addition to your team. Also, your percentages can increase when hitting against a pitcher from the opposite side of the plate.

Q A boy in seventh grade is 6 feet tall and a strong right-handed hitter. Should he be tutored to be a switch-hitter?
George

A If an athlete can be strong and coordinated from both sides of his body—that is, ambidextrous—he could have an advantage in any sport. If he can readily adapt to various basic tasks, as well as baseball-specific movements, then work with him—and more power to him!

It's a good challenge, and if he makes it to the major leagues, he'll certainly be more valuable.

Strategies for improving your batting

Q What's the best way for me to improve my batting?
Joseph, 10

A I recommend that you do some of the following with some frequency:

First, read some books with illustrations on hitting. Then, work with a knowledgeable, skilled coach or instructor one on one. Practice in a batting cage. The emphasis should be not on regular practice, but on perfect practice, until you develop that good form and muscle memory.

When you have time, get together with your baseball pals around the neighborhood and make up games where you hit baseballs from a tee. Swing a stick at a rubber ball. Play strikeout up

My Pitch

BUNTS COUNT, TOO: To reach 3,000 hits, even a slugger needs a few bunt hits.

ASSOCIATED PRESS

against a wall or any game that you can create that helps you with your agility, quickness, muscle-memory, strength, anticipation or simple love of the game.

 What's the best pitch to swing at to get a home run?

Matt, 10

A A ball coming in straight—or a fastball, as it's commonly known—that's the pitch players practice swinging at most frequently. Fastballs are easier to time, and it's easier to keep your balance while swinging at the pitch.

Picking a home run pitch

Breaking out of a slump

 What's your best advice for helping a hitter get out of a slump?
Andrew, 15

A Well, you're asking the resident expert here, because every year I go through at least one or two serious slumps. Remember, though, that advice is easy to give, but hard to follow.

First, think positive. Don't ever call it a slump—call it a period of adjustment.

Then, remember: No one is good or on top of his game all the time. Next, consider that you might be helped by more "correct" practice, making sure you're doing all the right things the right way. Or maybe it would help to take a day off to clear your mind.

You need to learn why you're temporarily having problems: Is the pitcher better? Are the pitchers making good pitches on you? Are you injured? Or is the law of averages catching up with you and bringing your performance back down to earth?

Once you know the cause of your problem, there are specific ways to solve the temporary difficulties.

Timing the pitch

 I'm always a second or two late when I swing the bat. How can I fix this?
Ben, 11

A Well, Ben, I have an either/or answer to your question.

If you desire to play baseball at a higher level, then try modifying your stance to an open one where your hands are closer to the hitting area. Then practice swinging a bat quickly—not for power, because that's when you tighten up the body and actually swing slower than usual.

If, over time, you find that your muscles and

My Pitch

skills do not enable you to hit the ball at advanced levels—where the ball reaches the plate in 0.4 or 0.5 seconds—then consider switching to slow-pitch softball, where you may become king of the hill.

Q **Rod Carew once claimed that when he was in a hitting groove, he could see the seams on a baseball coming toward him. Did that ever happen to you?**
Michael, 13

Focus on fastballs

A Some players, like Carew, might have picked up on the spin on a baseball —but for the most part, most players (myself included) key off a variety of other things in their approaches to hitting. For instance, I suggest anticipating a fastball, then making adjustments for a breaking ball or off-speed pitch.

HITTING GROOVE: Rod Carew

ASSOCIATED PRESS

Q **Why do so many players take the first pitch when it so often seems to be a strike? What's the theory behind not swinging at it?**
Rick

Casing a pitcher

A Baseball players are probably split down the middle on their practice of swinging at the first pitch or of letting it go.

Some of baseball's best hitters—Ted Williams, for instance—will tell you that you can learn many things from letting the first pitch go. Many times, you can determine the velocity, movement or location of a pitcher's delivery.

Talking Baseball

**LAST TO HIT .400:
Ted Williams**

ASSOCIATED PRESS

A good hitter does not worry about hitting with one or two strikes. The belief is that the more pitches you see from a guy, the more you know about him that will help you get a hit or coax a walk. The best hitters don't follow that routine of letting the first pitch go every time at bat, though.

Finding a comfortable hitting stance

Q **What's the best kind of stance I can use at the plate to be a good hitter?**

Andy, 11

A Over the years, I've seen good hitters use all kinds of stances—open, straight up, closed . . . Rod Carew, for instance, used an open

My Pitch

stance. Harmon Killebrew had more of a straight-up stance. Roberto Clemente's stance was extremely closed.

My advice to any young person just learning the game is to try them all. See what's comfortable. Practice long and hard to see which one serves you best. There's one thing for certain: The way you first begin to bat is not the way you will hit later on in life.

PIONEER PRESS FILE PHOTO

3,000 CLUB MEMBER: Roberto Clemente

Q What advice do you have for kids who want to learn how to pull the ball?

Peter, 10

A To pull the ball, a batter must concentrate on getting the head of the bat through the strike zone, angled toward left field if you're right-handed and toward right field if you're left-handed.

I recommend standing a little closer to the plate. Then, when balls are delivered over the plate as strikes, you can move your front foot toward the base line, enabling you to pull the ball more frequently.

Q What advice do you have on learning to pull the ball?

B.J., 13

Q How do you generate so much power in your swing?

Chris, 9

A When it comes to pulling the ball, you can try a couple of strategies. You can stand closer to the plate and use an open stance. Or you

Pulling the ball

More on pulling the ball and power swings

Talking Baseball

Talking to your coach

can try using a lighter bat to enable you to get the head of the bat on the ball before it reaches home plate.

In terms of generating power, remember that power comes from bat quickness and physical strength. Therefore, try to build up both.

Q **How do you talk to a coach who doesn't let all of his players play in a game?**

Geoff

ASSOCIATED PRESS

LEARNING THE GAME: Little League baseball is a time to test your talents and stretch your abilities.

My Pitch

A I would suggest that you ask to talk to the coach after a game or on a day off. Then you can find out about your playing possibilities or his team's strategy. Asking questions shows that you are ready to learn. A coach usually will talk to a youngster who is interested in learning, if not playing.

If we are talking Little League here, I would hope the coach believes in letting all of his players play at some time or another and not be concerned with winning at all costs.

Q I'm discouraged about baseball because I'm the worst player on our team. What should I do?

Rick

Assessing your talent

A Speaking honestly and openly to you, I suggest that if you truly love the game and the competition, choose one of these options, if you think it might apply to you: Participate in baseball until you feel that you physically cannot keep up. Then, perhaps choose another team sport or an individual sport—anything from field hockey to long-distance running.

Then, if you find that playing sports is not your thing, you still can be one of the fans. Finally, as you get older, you can fix them all by setting your goal on becoming a successful businessperson and purchasing your own franchise. You can be the owner of a team and maybe get just as much fulfillment and satisfaction.

Q I have a friend who is scared of the baseball. Do you have any tips for him?

Kenneth, 11

Overcoming fear of the ball

Talking Baseball

A If a person wants to play competitive baseball at any level, he or she cannot be afraid of being hit by the ball when it's pitched or hit.

To overcome his fear, your friend can play games and practice with one of the softer, hard-rubber regulation-size balls that are manufactured today.

With these balls, you can learn to duck or turn away from a pitched ball that's too close. You also can get used to being hit by the ball in an effort to overcome this fear, which lurks in the back of all hitters' minds.

Supervising young pitchers

Q What is a good age for a kid to start pitching?

Peter, 9

A Whenever you start playing Little League baseball, it's probably OK to start to pitch. The important thing is having a concerned, observant adult—whether it's a parent or the coach—who can supervise the number of pitches you throw and make sure that there's adequate rest in between the times you go to the mound to pitch.

When you first start pitching, remember: No breaking pitches that can hurt the arm.

Parents, do not let a kid hurt himself to win at all costs. That cost may be too high. A big win today may hurt the development of the arm and, perhaps, prevent a shot at a scholarship or a major-league career.

Athletic stamina hard to maintain

Q I was on a traveling softball team, and I got tired playing during our two-month season. How can you put in so much time over a whole season and not get worn out?

Julie, 15

My Pitch

A The truth is, no matter what kind of shape professional ballplayers are in, every athlete who plays every day over the course of a season (162 games plus almost 30 spring training games) gets worn out physically and mentally. If you could be a fly on the wall in the average training room in September and see all the tape jobs, ice packs, therapy and rehab sessions going on, you'd have your best view of this sport.

Chapter 2

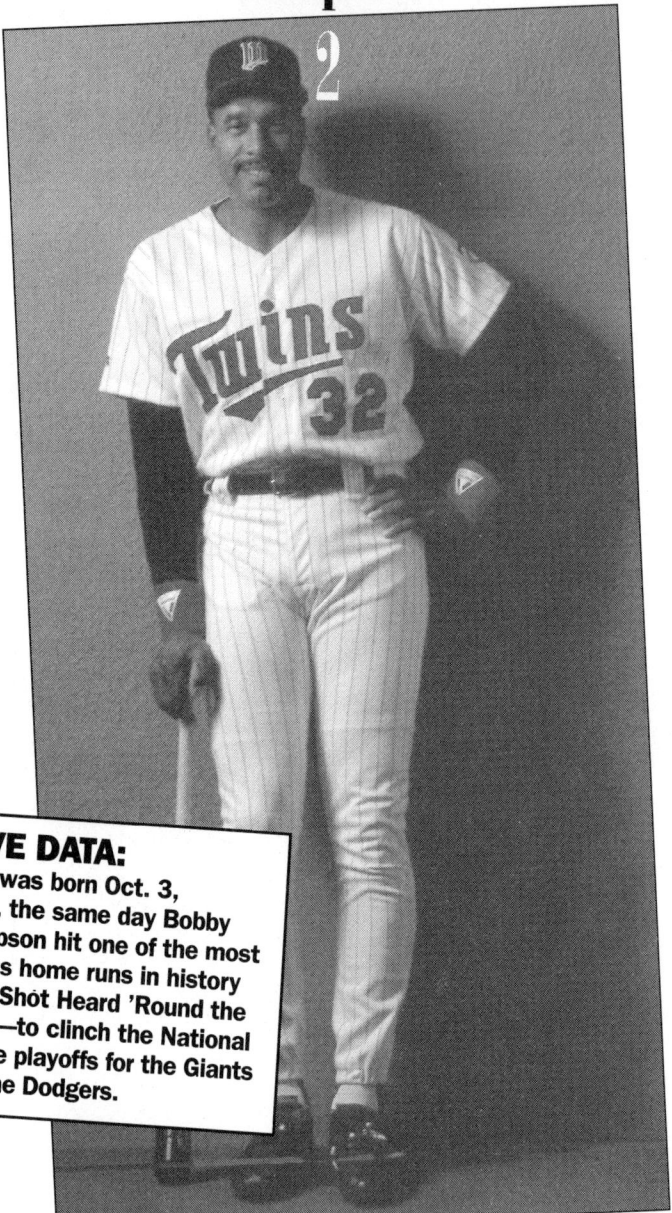

DAVE DATA:
Dave was born Oct. 3, 1951, the same day Bobby Thompson hit one of the most famous home runs in history —the Shot Heard 'Round the World—to clinch the National League playoffs for the Giants over the Dodgers.

JIM ARNDT

STANDING TALL: Dave's a big man with big opinions.

MY TURN at Bat

Q In your career, which National League and which American League pitcher were the toughest to hit against?

Clifford

Tough choice picking toughest pitchers

A Gee, I've faced so many tough pitchers—from Tom Seaver and Bob Gibson to Steve Carlton and Juan Marichal—it's hard to single out one. But for the toughest pitcher in the National League, I guess I'll go with the Houston Astros' James Rodney Richard.

He no longer pitches, but he was 6 feet 8 1/2 inches and 250 pounds, and he could hold five baseballs in one hand. He was clocked throwing 100 mph during the 1980 All-Star Game in Los Angeles.

ASSOCIATED PRESS

AMONG THE TOUGHEST: A brushback pitch from Nolan Ryan prompts Dave to rush the mound.

PIONEER PRESS FILE PHOTO

FIREBALLER: The Astros' James Rodney Richard was clocked at 100 mph during the 1980 All-Star Game.

In the American League, my nod goes to Nolan Ryan, because he's been consistently as tough as anyone. I finally hit my first home run against him in 1992 and—would you believe—a storm blew into Arlington Stadium and rained out the game.

Baseball's best team

Q What's the best team you've been on?
Justin, 8

A The 1992 Toronto Blue Jays team would be hard to top. It took more than $40 million to bring all that talent together, but it also took every bit of that team's talent to go all the way in 1992. The 1981 New York Yankees—Reggie Jackson, Ron Guidry and Goose Gossage, etc.—would rank a very close second.

Best and worst stadiums

Q What are your favorite and least favorite stadiums to play in?
Jesse, 16

A In the National League, I probably least liked San Francisco's Candlestick Park, because it was always cold and windy, and very few fans would attend the games. San Diego, my home park then, had the best climate—and field, despite its high fence.

In the American League, the SkyDome in Toronto is the most extraordinary place to play. My least favorite park probably would be Texas, because it gets so hot and humid there in midsummer.

Spring training is warm-up time

Q Why does spring training sometimes go kind of hard for you while you usually have such a good start in the regular season?
John

A I, like many other veterans, use spring training as a time for gradual preparation for the championship season, when it counts. Although players would like to win every game they play and perform well, they try to pace themselves for the long season ahead and not expend all their physical, mental and emotional skills in spring training. After those 30 games, there are 162 more to go! But when the bell rings—when the season starts— I'm always ready.

 Why don't pro baseball players shake hands with opposing teams, like hockey players do?
Anonymous

Baseball customs

Each sport has its own customs and traditions. From the early days of baseball, players were not only fierce competitors—but sometimes enemies. As recently as five or six years ago, if a player shook hands with an opposing player before the game, some managers would fine their own players.

Today, players are much more friendly (with free agency, many of us have been teammates at some point in our careers), but it's still not like the Stanley Cup finals.

 How do you celebrate after a game when you've hit a home run?
William, 11

Home run celebrations

I don't have any particular ritual. Part of it depends on what kind of home run it was— but not as much as what kind of game it was.

After a loss, I can't get excited. But after a win, at our postgame meal, I might be prone to talk a little trash if I hit a home run off a pitcher I have something against. More often, I'll sit quietly with a cool drink and savor the moment. I've done both, though.

Talking Baseball

After 3,000, what next?

Q Now that you've reached 3,000 hits, what's your next goal in baseball?
Greg, 8

A My goal every year is to win a championship. Without this vision, I don't think I'd play very well. I don't really set individual career goals; whatever numbers I end up with when I finish playing are what I end up with. I've played so long now that I seem to reach another plateau every couple of at-bats. But personal goals can take away from a team effort.

Being there for teammates

Q If you saw a teammate doing something illegal, what would you do?
Andrea, 10, and Brian, 11

A It would be important for me to pull him aside and talk to him. I would let him know that, at least, I know what he is doing. I would try to find out the real reason he's doing these things, and I would explain to him the consequences of his actions.

I don't know if anyone else would bring it to his attention, but I would not want any teammate of mine to lose his job, his family, freedom, health or life over something illegal—not if I could help it.

Valuable baseball memorabilia

Q How much is your rookie card worth?
Bobbie, 9

A I honestly don't know. I do know that there are more than 250 kinds of cards and other memorabilia that have been produced about me since my rookie year in 1973. They range from tote bags and ceramic statues to silver-minted coins.

I do know a player's popularity and accomplishments help determine whether those memorabilia are worth something later on. Since all kids cannot be investors or business people, I suggest that you collect memorabilia of your favorite players for the enjoyment of it.

 What do you think the effect of rapidly escalating salaries will be on baseball?

Tim

Pro salary squeeze

 For the players, salaries will not grow as fast or as much as they have in the past five years. The stars will get paid, but the marginal players probably will be squeezed out of the game.

But if baseball is resourceful and sells the game to the fans and community in better and different ways than in the past, then it won't have to rely only on TV money and/or raising ticket prices to keep good players on the team. When teams are resourceful, they don't rely only on a farm system or totally on free agents to build a team.

Where did you like playing best—Toronto, California, San Diego or the Twin Cities?

Jim

Favorite home team city

There was good and bad in all the cities I played in. San Diego had great weather—and a bad team! The California Angels were similar. Even in New York, we had good teams playing in a tough city—and the management there was antagonistic.

By far, in Toronto, I had the best of all worlds. When the weather was good, officials would open the roof of the SkyDome. In bad weather, they would close it. And, of course, in Toronto, we won it all in 1992.

I like being home in the Twin Cities, and I hope for good things here.

Good sportsmanship

Q Why were the Toronto Blue Jays rather sore winners after the 1992 World Series last year by pulling that ungracious tomahawk chop and war chant in the locker room? Isn't that sending a poor message to youth regarding sportsmanship?
Kelly, 21

A The Blue Jays faced the tomahawk chop and the war chant virtually everywhere they went in Atlanta—from the airport runways to the shopping malls to the stadium itself. In celebrating the championship, they felt it was a fun reaction to overcoming the challenge at the moment, rather than being disrespectful to the ball club, the players or Indian culture.

To a man, every player on the Blue Jays would say that not only were the Braves good players and great competitors, but they would compliment the Atlanta fans and management as extending nothing but friendliness and hospitality to us during our time in town.

On the issue of sportsmanship, I hope that the young people watching did not take that as an insensitive gesture toward a defeated team, because there are proper ways to deal with victory as well as defeat.

CUT DOWN: The only thing that could stop the Atlanta fans' tomahawk chop was opposing teams' victories.

ASSOCIATED PRESS

Baseball's minority hiring record

Q What is your view of baseball's track record on hiring black managers and front-office personnel?
           Matt, 18

A In 1987, only 2 percent of baseball's front-office positions were filled by minorities. In 1993, 17 percent of those jobs were filled by minorities, and there were five minority managers in baseball. All these areas can still be improved, and I would hope that they would be. I think that it would just help the entire game of baseball.

AL vs. NL

Q What's the biggest difference between playing in the American League and the National League?
           Pat, 14

A Probably the biggest difference is that umpires move the game along more quickly in the National League. Frequently, National League games tend to be shorter.

Asian player breakthrough

Q How long do you think it will be before there are any Asian-American or Hmong baseball players in the major leagues?
      Ann, a teacher of English as a Second Language, on behalf of her kindergarten through third-grade Hmong students

A As you know, for all the millions of kids who play baseball for fun, only a small fraction go on to play in the big leagues. Therefore, with the Asian-American and Hmong community small in terms of the overall U.S. population, it might take quite a few years for that to happen.

    I certainly hope that one of your students will have the desire, skill, ability, luck and courage to be the first. I'll be pulling for them!

Talking Baseball

One more turn as pitcher

Q Have you ever wished you'd get a chance to try your old curveball from your pitching days for an inning or two in a major-league game?
— Bob Sr. and Bob Jr.

CHANGING BY DEGREES: Slugger Dave was a pitcher throughout his college years.

A Over the course of the last few years with the teams I've played for, I have made it no secret that if they ever needed me to go to the mound for an inning or two, I would welcome that opportunity. In my case, I'm sure they know I could mop up if the occasion arose, but they have always been afraid of my being injured.

Unfortunately, the events of the past year show that you can be hurt on the mound. Recently, a pitcher was hit in the forehead and ended up being carried off the field on a stretcher. Also last year, the Texas Rangers' Jose Canseco hurt his arm during such a short pitching stint. As a result, he missed the rest of the season and put his career in jeopardy. Events like these lessen my chances of pitching any time soon.

Baseball's tobacco controversy

Q What do you think of the tobacco-ban controversy in major-league baseball?
— Jesse, 12

A Major-league baseball should have a comprehensive, iron-clad drug policy in place before it singles out tobacco. Baseball needs a program that helps athletes through education and prevention strategies, treatment and privacy—and one that eliminates offenders.

My Turn at Bat

It's a good move for baseball to work to improve its image among youths and the rest of the country by taking a leadership stance on issues like these. Whatever guidelines emerge should not be wishy-washy.

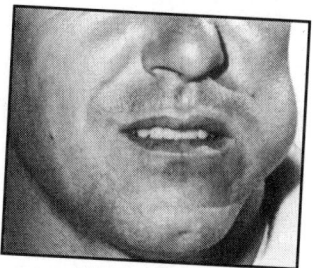

PIONEER PRESS FILE PHOTO

SPITTIN' IMAGE: Baseball players' tobacco use is just one element of an overall drug policy that Dave would like to see addressed.

Finally, I will go on record predicting that major-league baseball will attempt to negotiate with the players to put some type of comprehensive drug and tobacco policy in place, but I don't think it will happen until 1998.

Q What was the hardest thing for you to learn about playing baseball?
Erica

Toughest thing about baseball

A Since baseball was always something I wanted to do and was pretty good at, I would say the hardest thing for me to do was learning to hit the ball well. That is the part of the game into which I've put the most effort.

To hit a fast-moving, round ball with a rounded stick while nine men try to prevent you from getting on base might be the toughest thing to do in all of sports. Once you think you've got a hitting style down pat, you lose it, so you continually have to try to improve your skills in this area.

Q What do you think of the salaries professional athletes make? Are they fair in terms of what athletes offer society?
Stephanie, 14, and Burt, 12

Fairness of pro sports salaries

A First, you see, I started playing professional baseball at a time when we were paid very little and had a very minor package of pension and medical benefits. In those days, we would look for off-season work to make ends meet.

In my career, I've bridged that time to the contracts of today, when a player can secure the future for himself and his family, and I think that's really great. I also think most fans would be happy for each person who could do this if it were they or a family member.

Second, the fairness of a player's salary in relation to his contribution to society should not be tied together, because professional sports is simply entertainment for people—and what people pay today for entertainment and leisure varies widely.

Dealing with size is a tall order

Q: Is it an advantage or disadvantage to be so tall when you're batting, and why?
Tom, 15

A: I've thought about and been asked this question throughout my career. The answer for me is: both. Being 6-foot-6 with long legs, I believe my strike zone is bigger than most players', so I've had to cover more area than a smaller guy would. That's a disadvantage.

The advantage for me is that I've been blessed with strength and reflexes to assist me when I attack the ball in the strike zone. Now the fun and beautiful part of this game is that people with a wide range of sizes and abilities can all be successful.

Reds owner has left poor legacy

Q: What's your opinion of Cincinnati Reds owner Marge Schott?
Ben, 13

A: I do not know her personally, have never met her and have only heard her preferences and opinions about a few topics. Since she is a person

My Turn at Bat

who can and does influence the lives of many people and the image of the sport we love, I personally hope that even at this stage of her life that she could learn to change and be truly accepting of all people and turn around the negative legacy she has perpetuated within our sport. Prejudice and discrimination at any level are not acceptable and should not be condoned.

Q **What do you think of women playing in major-league sports, and do you think they should?**
Crystal, 13, and Heather

Women in pro sports

A I probably walk a fine line here when I say that today it would be very hard for a woman, physically, to handle the rigors of professional baseball, basketball or football—no gimmicks—as an everyday performer. I do not rule it out in the future, though.

As of today, women's leagues are a much more likely place for women to perform at the professional level.

ASSOCIATED PRESS

SEPARATE WAYS: 1994 will mark the debut of the Silver Bullets, an all-female professional baseball team that will compete against an all-male minor-league team.

Talking Baseball

Favorite managers

Who's your favorite manager in baseball?
Brian, 11

In my long career, I've probably had more managers than any other player. One of my early favorites was John McNamara of the San Diego Padres. He communicated well with his players and gave me my first chance to play every day.

Among more recent managers, the Toronto Blue Jays' Cito Gaston—whom I've known for so long—would be my pick. We not only played together in San Diego when I first started, but we shared the thrill of our first World Championship.

PIONEER PRESS FILE PHOTO
EARLY FAVORITE: John McNamara

ASSOCIATED PRESS
RECENT FAVORITE: Cito Gaston

Room for minor league teams, too

What do you think of the new St. Paul Saints?
B.J., 13

Bravo, Saints! I think it's great to have a new minor-league baseball team in town. It's great entertainment for families, someplace where youngsters literally can reach out and touch and identify with players.

My Turn at Bat

Some young people may not know this, but in the old days (pre-Twins), the Twin Cities actually had two teams—the Minneapolis Millers and the Saints. Today, the metropolitan area is large enough to support both major-league and minor-league baseball.

Q: As a native of St. Paul, what did you think of the North Stars moving out?
Troy

A: I heard the news while I was in Florida for 1993 spring training. I thought, "No way!" But it's true. Although I've only attended a few games in person, like any sports fan, I've pulled for them over the years. It will be hard to imagine a first-class region like Minnesota—a hockey haven—not having a professional team to represent it.

Hockey franchise farewell

Chapter 3

DAVE DATA:
In 1992, at age 41, Dave becomes the oldest player to drive in 100 runs in a season.

RICH MARSHALL/**ST. PAUL PIONEER PRESS**

GOLD GLOVER: Spring training is the time when veterans like Dave and the rawest of rookies concentrate on baseball fundamentals and conditioning.

INSIDE Baseball

Q: What's it like being a professional baseball player?
Elizabeth, 8

A: I am probably speaking for the approximately 700 athletes who play baseball at the major-league level: We really wouldn't want to do anything else for a living!

Our routine every day for 7 1/2 months and much of the off-season is very physical. You have to play hurt, sick, tired—and when things aren't going your way.

But, in return, you are treated to first-class travel, food, hotels and entertainment, and people recognize you everywhere. Of course, there is a good side and a bad side to fame and fortune, but without a doubt, there's a lot more good than bad.

Q: At what age did you start playing pro ball, and with what club?
Dorothy

A: I started my professional career at age 21 with the San Diego Padres. I was drafted out

A baseball player's life

Pro debut

ASSOCIATED PRESS

HIGH HOPES: Early in his career with the San Diego Padres, Dave talks about his love for the game and what it takes to succeed long-term.

Changing positions

of the University of Minnesota in June and turned 22 after my first season in October.

Q When you pitched in 1964, your team won the St. Paul City Midget League championship. When did you change positions?
Lillian, 70

A I don't remember the year, but I changed positions at different times during my formative years. That's something I would recommend to all kids playing the sport, because you never know what position you will grow into.

I started as a third baseman in Peewees. Then I became a shortstop and pitcher in Midgets. In college, I pitched and played outfield. Today, I'm a designated hitter and play outfield and first base. Who knows—before I'm done, maybe they'll let me pitch an inning.

Ranking the years

Q What level of baseball play was the most fun—Little League, high school, college or pros—and why?
Cris, 10

A Professionally, I would say that 1992—No. 19 of professional baseball, with the World Series win—was the most fun. After that, I would say my Little League years, where I was learning and playing every day after school and in the summer. We seemed to never get tired. I wish I could say that today!

Influential managers

Q Of all your major-league managers, which one influenced you the most?
A.J., 10

A In terms of managers, I would choose John McNamara, who gave me my first chance at

Inside Baseball

becoming a starter for the San Diego Padres. Being able to talk to him a lot helped me gain a great deal of comfort at the major-league level.

Q **Who do you think is the best baseball player (except you)?**
Ryan, 11

Baseball's best

A I've played so long that I know that no one is ever "the best" for long—maybe for a moment or maybe one or two years in a row.

In my career, I've seen guys who were the best for a while—like Willie Mays, Hank Aaron, Pete Rose, Joe Morgan, Jose Canseco (with his 40-40 season of home runs and stolen bases), Kirby Puckett or maybe even Barry Bonds today.

PIONEER PRESS FILE PHOTO
100% CLUB: Barry Bonds always gives his all.

A bit of advice to those who reach for greatness in any field: Be the best that you can be, and that alone can make you happy.

Q **Whom do you most admire in baseball, and who has had the greatest impact on your career?**
Lisa, 11

Most admired in baseball

A This was not an easy question for me, and my answer tells you something about how I view my peers. First, I'd use another word in conjunction with "admire," and that is "respect." When I play against an opponent, I have no time

Changes in baseball

really to admire him—only to respect him. When I play on the same team as that person, then I can step back and admire what he does or contributes to the team.

My criteria for viewing a player this way are: He must have a positive influence and set a good example; he must have a good work ethic—and get good results.

Over the years, the people I've known who fit in this category are too numerous to list here.

Second, I thought long and hard about who had the greatest impact on my career and found that I couldn't arrive at a clear-cut answer on my baseball career. But in the bigger picture, out of the dozen or so people I considered, I would have to choose my mother. As a single parent, she had the most direct impact on my life, enabling me to succeed in any career I chose.

Q How much has professional baseball changed since you began playing?
Michael, 15

A Quite a bit, but I'd say it's changed a lot more off the field than on it. Between the lines, the game is played similarly to when I began—only the heroes' names are different.

The major differences off the field involve how athletes today physically prepare for each season with weightlifting, cross-training, etc. Medical and surgical treatment and repair are miles ahead today. Also, the salaries are much different.

Today, there also is an abundance of TV and cable coverage, where you can see games and get to know the players much better. We were very seldom televised back then.

Inside Baseball

Q: What do you think about when you're at the plate?
Erin, 9, and Ann, 12

Thoughts at the plate

A: When the pitcher delivers the ball toward home plate, I think about hitting the ball hard where the outfielders aren't. That's the simplest way to answer your question.

But I also know that to get good, consistent results at home plate, I have to use the information I've gathered long before stepping into the batter's box—like reading the scouting report or, from the bench, seeing how many different pitches the guy has.

I also consider specific factors that are different each game: Is the ball moving? How is the opposing team positioned to defend against me? This information can make the task of getting a hit against the nine-men-to-one odds a little easier.

Q: What's your favorite baseball memory?
Eric, 11

Favorite memories of the game

A: My favorite memory: In 1992, hugging my Toronto teammates and falling dead-tired in a pile in the middle of a totally silent Atlanta-Fulton County Stadium after we won the World Series. The feeling is so special when it's the first time and you have triumphed going against the tide.

Q: What's your favorite memory of a player you played with or against?
Marty

Favorite memories of a player

A: I have witnessed so many special events or moments in my long career that it's hard to choose. I remember Hank Aaron's home runs as he

Talking Baseball

MVP DAYS: What a pleasure watching Don Mattingly set records.

PIONEER PRESS FILE PHOTO

approached Babe Ruth's all-time record, and I was there when Lou Brock broke the all-time single-season stolen-base record.

But my most special memory is my Yankee teammate Don Mattingly setting records in 1985, his American League MVP year. Among other things, he hit six grand slams in one season and a home run on eight consecutive days—very special accomplishments.

Pregame rituals

Q Do you have any unusual pregame rituals or superstitions you follow?
Melissa, 11

A I have seen players do everything from burn incense and chant to read Scriptures. Others dress for a game piece by piece in a specific order, don't change undergarments during a good streak, eat or drink a specific food on game day and do their stretch and exercise routines at precise times. But I don't have any superstitions or pregame rituals that I follow.

Three-homer game

Q What's the most home runs you've ever hit in one game?
Brian, 11

A The most is three. I did it on April 13, 1991, against the Minnesota Twins at the Metrodome when I was playing for the California Angels. Maybe that's why the Twins signed me!

Inside Baseball

Q: Have you ever played any practical jokes on your teammates, and what were they?
Josh, 12, and Jess, 10

A: Maybe I'm just kind of square, but my jokes are usually verbal, not physical ones. I've seen hundreds of practical jokes played on other guys—from a player giving a teammate a hot foot, to shaving cream hidden in the shower towels, to rubber snakes placed in players' shoes. Through it all, though, I'm usually just a spectator.

Practical jokes

Q: Do you ever get depressed during a batting slump or a team losing streak?
Missy, 13

A: Yes. I'm just like any other professional athlete. We've all got feelings, and we all want to contribute, win, play our best and the like. Even after so many years, I try not to take out my frustrations on friends and family, but the truth is, they feel it from me, too.

Battling a batting slump

Q: Who is your favorite competitor in baseball?
Matthew, 10

A: Probably Barry Bonds of the San Francisco Giants. Although I've never played against him, I've known him and his dad, Bobby, for many years—even before Barry became a professional ballplayer. I like the way he has applied himself to the game and excelled. He deserves a lot of wins in seasons to come.

Favorite competitors

Q: Have you ever hurt yourself while hitting your cleats with the bat?
Andrea, 15, and Jim

Baseball habits

▲43▲

A No, I haven't. That's a habit I developed over time to knock the dirt from my cleats. But now, when I DH most of the time on synthetic carpet, needless to say, there really isn't much dirt.

But I intend to keep following the habits and patterns I've used over the years when I've been successful.

Earflap flap

Q Why don't you wear earflaps on your batting helmet, like most players?

Amy, 16

A When I began playing in 1973, it was optional what kind of helmet you wore—with a flap or without. I was more comfortable without the flap. Today, all athletes entering major league baseball since the late '70s must wear an earflap.

Embarrassing moments

Q What's the most embarrassing thing that ever happened to you during a game, and what did you do about it?

Lisa, 11

A Over the years, there have been many embarrassing things that happened to me, but I try to keep them to a minimum.

The worst: One day I was playing center field for the San Diego Padres when there was a base hit to center with the runner from second base trying to score. The second baseman lined up for the cutoff throw. But when I threw the ball, my foot slipped on the wet field. He ducked, but the ball hit him right in the backside. Every player on the field laughed at me. Of course, I was embarrassed, but I had to take it and keep on playing.

Inside Baseball

Q: What's your favorite part of baseball?
JoAnn

Favorite thing in baseball

A: There are many parts of the game that rank right near the top—like the salary I make or the recognition I get. But when I think of how physically fit and healthy I am, compared with others my age, I give baseball the credit.

Q: How many inside-the-park home runs have you hit in your career?
Brian

Inside-the-park homers

A: Believe it or not, out of my 450-plus home runs, only one has been an inside-the-park homer. I got that on a wet, muddy field at old Comiskey Park in Chicago in, I believe, 1981.

I hit a towering drive to left center. The ball hit the wall and caromed toward center field. By the time the outfielders retrieved it, I had rounded the bases, but I needed a head-first slide to make it home safely.

Q: Do players buy their own bats, or are they provided by the team?
Peter, 10

Bat buying

A: The team purchases the bats for the players. But each player finds the style, model, weight and bat company he prefers. The team then makes periodic orders from approximately six bat companies.

Q: What was it like playing against your former team, the Toronto Blue Jays?
Melinda, 13

Blue Jays reunion

Talking Baseball

A To tell you the truth, since I missed the 1993 spring-training match-ups, I was very distracted during that first meeting in Toronto when I reunited with my former teammates.

With all the media coverage, the hellos, the fantastic outpouring from the fans and city, honestly, I wasn't good for much during that first series.

Baseball signals

Q Can you tell the Twins what the Blue Jays' signals mean?

Ted, 10

A Since passing signals from the manager or coach to the players is a critical part of each game, knowing your opponent's signs and sharing them with your teammates could short-circuit the other team's game plan. Occasionally, this information is shared with a new team.

But to prevent this kind of secret-sharing, which can affect a team's chances, your former team frequently will change the signals to be used against you. I find that the kind of information more frequently shared deals with the opposing manager's or players' tendencies, strengths and weaknesses.

"Playing" baseball

Q Is your love of baseball so great that you'd be willing to play for free?

Dean, 13

A From the first day you walk onto a baseball diamond—through Little League, through high school and college and even senior leagues—you call it "playing baseball." But the first day you draw a paycheck to perform on the baseball field, it should no longer be mistakenly called "playing

Inside Baseball

BUZZ MAGNUSON/ST. PAUL PIONEER PRESS

TOWER OF STRENGTH: As a high-school senior at St. Paul Central, Dave towered over the rest of the 1969 All-City Conference baseball team.

baseball." It then becomes a business, a way of earning a living.

I've been fortunate to earn a living for the past 20-plus years doing something I love. I don't think, though, that I would work this hard at this age for free.

Chapter 4

DAVE DATA:
The first athlete drafted in three professional sports, Dave is one of only 19 players to reach 3,000 hits.

RICH MARSHALL/ST. PAUL PIONEER PRESS

HISTORIC SWING: Dave connects for No. 3,000 on Sept. 16, 1993.

PERSONAL
Milestones

Q What's it like being in the 3,000 Hit Club?
                                            Kevin

3,000 Hit Club

A I'm proud to be in such elite company, and I consider it one of my greatest achievements. And the biggest reason why? Because, despite all the good things people now say about me being a pretty good hitter, it was only a few years ago that some of these same people didn't believe that I could still play, let alone accomplish something like this.

Q As you neared your 3,000th hit, did you find that you were more nervous at the plate?
                                            Amber, 9

Coping with pressure

Q Was it hard getting all the extra attention as you neared 3,000 hits?
                                Bobby, Chet and Crystal

A The truth is, I thought that the focus and all the media attention would add up to being a positive thing for me if I could keep it in check. I don't think I was able to handle the individual focus as well as I would have liked to.

I found myself getting pretty cranky when I

Talking Baseball

HIT PARADE: Baseballs in their bags detail Dave's quest for No. 3,000.
BILL ALKOFER/ST. PAUL PIONEER PRESS

wasn't reaching the milestone as quickly as I would have liked to or had planned.

I think that impatient is a better word to describe my feelings, rather than plain old nervous.

In terms of all the extra attention, yes, it was kind of hard. The tremendous amount of coverage of the event—covering everything from my boyhood to my entire professional life—almost every day for about three weeks took some time away from my physical and mental preparation for the game.

After it was over, I welcomed the extensive coverage of the journey and the milestone itself.

Historic moment

Q What's your favorite thing you've done in baseball?

Mark, 7

A My favorite thing was to get the game-winning hit to cinch the World Series for the Blue Jays in 1992. And my favorite thing I did because of baseball was to buy my mother a fine home to live in that she enjoyed.

World series winning hit

Q How did it feel to get the winning hit in the 1992 World Series?

Tom

A It was really great for two main reasons. No. 1, I remember when I was very young play-

Personal Milestones

ing in the sandlots—my brother and I—every practice we would always say, "You're the man up, men on base, two outs, last game of the World Series . . . here's the pitch."

We always tried to get that hit to win the game for our team, and finally, I was that man—that key man—up at bat at the right time, and I got the hit, so it was beautiful.

No. 2, I felt so good because I had prepared myself for this situation every day every year to do something like this. It was fabulous. So it wasn't luck. It was preparation meeting opportunity.

ASSOCIATED PRESS

TEAMWORK: Individual records aside, the career high point for Dave was the Toronto Blue Jays' 1992 World Series victory.

Q How did it feel to pass Babe Ruth on the all-time hit list?

Nathan, 13, and Russell, 10

Passing Babe Ruth

A It was a great feeling. To be compared with Babe Ruth in any way (except his stomach) is quite exciting for me. It was a huge accomplishment.

NICKOLAS MURAY

GOOD COMPANY: Passing Babe Ruth on the all-time hit list was a special accomplishment.

51

Talking Baseball

Looking ahead

Q When you're elected to the Hall of Fame, in which team's uniform do you want to be portrayed?

Richie, 9, and Sam, 12

A I appreciate everyone's talk about my reaching a very special place for baseball players who have finished their playing careers. But I will never assume I'm guaranteed—or have earned—a place there. We'll wait and see what happens after I retire.

Needless to say, I haven't given any thought to what uniform I might choose.

WINFIELD FOUNDATION

TREASURED TROPHIES: Gold Gloves and silver bats pay testimony to Dave's all-around baseball ability.

Weighing accomplishments

Q What would you like to accomplish in life in the years ahead, and what do you feel have been your biggest accomplishments so far?

Joseph, 12

A You've asked me maybe the toughest question so far. The best answer I can give is kind of general: I will continue to use the positive name and influence I've gained in sports to motivate and inspire other people in sports and business even after I stop playing baseball.

In terms of your second question, I would say this: To play the sport I love—and to reach the height of success as World Series champs—is very gratifying. But I'm also proud to be the person I am today, coming from St. Paul with no exact role model or road map to follow to achieve this.

First paycheck

Q How did you spend your very first paycheck as a professional baseball player?

Jock

Personal Milestones

A As best as I can recall, I bought a suit, shirt and tie to wear while traveling with the San Diego Padres. My first bonus check was invested in the stock market.

Q What's the longest home run you ever hit—where and when?

Danny

Longest home run

A Some of my long home runs have been stopped by some part of the stadium—like the seats. But I do remember a home run I hit off Rick Sutcliffe in the mid-'80s at Yankee Stadium that landed at the feet of the guys in the bullpen. That's near the 500-foot mark.

Q What was your best year in baseball?

Jeff

Career year

A I'll answer your question from an individual perspective, not a team standpoint.

It's not a clear-cut choice, but I guess I'd choose 1979 with the San Diego Padres. I won a Gold Glove that year, led the league in RBIs with 118, hit .308 and had 34 home runs. All these numbers were very hard to achieve on a last-place team with the least-effective batting lineup in the National League.

In those days, they didn't give the Most Valuable Player award to guys on last-place teams.

Chapter 5

DAVE DATA:
In 1977, Dave leads the San Diego Padres with a 16-game hit streak and makes his first All-Star Game appearance, delivering the winning hit.

RICHARD MARSHALL/**ST. PAUL PIONEER PRESS**

FITTING IN: A veteran player like Dave has a lot of experience to share with Twins manager Tom Kelly's young team.

LIFE WITH the Twins

Q **Do you plan to finish your baseball career with the Minnesota Twins, and do you plan to live in Minnesota after you retire?**
Dave

A There is a good chance that the Twins might be the last team I play for, but I can only see down the road to the end of my contract after the '94 season. The relationships I develop and the opportunities that unfold will determine where I live after I stop playing. Whatever work I'm engaged in, I intend to enjoy that work.

But I would never retire and just do nothing. I plan to be very active and visible when I finish playing sports.

Q **How does it feel to be a Twin?**
Kinta

A I've noticed since becoming a Twin and spending more time in the Twin Cities that I attract a lot more attention than I did playing with other teams. Each game I play in the Metrodome, I try to make new friends and fans. I really enjoy providing entertainment and excitement to all the fans, especially when so many know me personally.

Beyond baseball

Dome field advantage

Talking Baseball

Coming home

Q Why did you want to join the Twins? What's it like to be back in the Twin Cities playing for the Twins?

Daniel, Tony, Rich, Nick, and Tanya

A Although my favorite team as a youngster growing up in St. Paul was the Twins, I never really had the chance to play for them because I was drafted by the San Diego Padres and signed with them. Then, of course, I played for New York, California and the Toronto Blue Jays. When I saw that I was not going to return to the World Champion Blue Jays this year, I took the initiative and gave the Twins a call, because I really thought it would be good to come home and play in front of friends and family after all these years.

I just thought it would be a great thing and exciting for me to play part of my career in the Twin Cities, so that one day when I retire, I can look back and say, "I did it! I played for those Twins!"

BILL ALKOFER/**ST. PAUL PIONEER PRESS**

HOMECOMING: Back in his hometown, Dave takes part in a publicity shoot.

K-I-R-B-Y!
K-I-R-B-Y!

Q Is Kirby Puckett your friend?

Andrea

Q Don't you get jealous when you see Kirby's popularity with the fans?

Bonnette, 10, St. Paul

Life with the Twins

A Kirby and I were friends even before I came to play for the Twins. Now we're even closer, because we get to do so many more things together. No, I'm not jealous when he gets the recognition he does, because he certainly deserves it. Just as I know for a fact that he's proud of me for all that I've done over the years and today. We're very happy for each other.

JOE ROSSI/ST. PAUL PIONEER PRESS

MUTUAL ADMIRATION SOCIETY: Dave and Twins superstar Kirby Puckett share baseball adventures and community involvement.

Team spirit

Q What's it like playing with Chuck Knoblauch, Kirby Puckett and all the other Twins stars?
Brad, 13

A Most of the guys are like younger brothers to me. I look at these guys as friends whom I truly respect, and I'm really glad that we don't have any guys on the team who are—if you know what I mean—a pain in the butt.

Dealing with age differences

Q What's it like being the oldest player on the Twins team?
Kathy

A As long as I play well, no one really cares about the difference in age. One thing for sure: When you play on a team with a lot of young guys, you have to keep your energy level up, and there's always a challenge to meet, so I like that a lot.

Making friends

Q When you came to the Twins, were you afraid you wouldn't make any friends?
Jordan, 10

Talking Baseball

A No. I wasn't afraid I wouldn't make friends, because I think I'm a pretty good guy—the kind of guy players think of as a friend. I did feel that it would take a while to get acquainted, because I only knew a few of my new teammates beforehand.

But once I got to telling stories of the old days, smiled and laughed with the boys, kept up with them in our workouts and played good baseball, I think we got along real well as the season rolled on.

Pressure from the fans

Q Did the fans put too much pressure on the Twins during their 1993 losing streaks?
Crystal, 12

A Because of so much media coverage, the fans of today are very knowledgeable—and opinionated—when it comes to judging the performance of their sports teams. As professional athletes, we have to take the good with the bad.

As a team, we did poorly much of the 1993 season. Consequently, much of the coverage was kind of negative. When the criticism gets hard on the players' ears and eyes, they usually stop reading the papers and watching the TV coverage. That's probably the best way to avoid having the criticism affect your performance and concentration.

Adjusting to a frustrating season

Q How frustrating was it to come from a winning team to one that didn't win as much?
Mark, 15

A It was really pretty frustrating. Although I know I made the best choice for me and my career in the long run, the first year after a championship season—with the prospects of a repeat—caused more than a bit of anxiety for me this season. A win-loss swing of about 40 games in one year was pretty difficult to endure.

▲58▲

Q **How long will it take you to hit your 500th home run?**

Nick

A If statistics from previous years—and my general health and well-being—hold pretty steady, I could reach that milestone at the end of my next two seasons (1995). I believe that physically I will be able to play that long, but I will try my best not to get hung up on playing for statistics. I haven't done that to date.

Another milestone ahead

DIRECT ROUTE: From his starring days on the University of Minnesota's Golden Gopher baseball team, Dave went straight to the major leagues to play with the San Diego Padres.

MY
Life

WINFIELD FOUNDATION

Chapter 1

DAVE DATA:
Dave was a pitcher until his final inning in college ball.

CHRIS POLYDOROFF/**ST. PAUL PIONEER PRESS**

FAMILY ROOTS: Dave attributes his success to the strong family values he and his brother, Steve, learned from their mother, Arline.

CHILDHOOD Memories

Baseball idols

Q: When you were growing up, who were your baseball idols, and what made you go into baseball?

Daniel, 11

A: Because I am a St. Paul native, my first idols were guys on the Twins, and we would imitate them in the sandlot all the time. There were guys like Harmon Killebrew—his swing—and Zoilo Versalles—his glove. And although I didn't see them on TV much, I liked guys like Bob Gibson, Willie Mays and Hank Aaron. I got to play against my idols, too.

I went into baseball because I had an older cousin who played—and because there was a playground a half block away from me. It was called Oxford Playground at the time—it's Jimmy Lee Recreation Center now.

PIONEER PRESS FILE PHOTO
HEROES: Slugger Willie Mays

PIONEER PRESS FILE PHOTO
HEROES: Pitcher Bob Gibson

ASSOCIATED PRESS
HEROES: Home-run king Hank Aaron

Young baseball fanatics

Once I started playing baseball, I took to it like a duck takes to water. I stayed with it because there were coaches, booster club members and interested parents who supported us and kept us interested in baseball, so it was a lot of fun.

Q: How much did you practice baseball as a kid?
Jake, Cottage Grove

A: As much as I could! Weather permitting, we played outdoors. Weather not permitting, we would practice indoors in the gym—our version of spring training. Even then, we would practice fielding, throwing, sliding and hitting, using rubber balls. By age 14, I started doing some weight training, too.

When not actually playing a baseball game, our small group of friends would create games, such as Strikeout, Home Run Derby and Tag Up. These often were games you could play with just two or three kids that focused on different facets of the game.

SMALL BEGINNINGS: Here's proof that Dave wasn't always a big guy: first-grader Dave at age 6.
WINFIELD FOUNDATION

Education always a priority

Q: What was your top priority as a kid—sports or education?
Dick, 9

A: In our household, you didn't do one without the other. My mother pushed the importance of an education. I knew I would pursue higher education even before I knew I wanted to be a professional baseball player. I loved sports, but only liked education. But I know that even when professional sports ends, education will continue—and help me throughout life.

Childhood Memories

Q Were you the best player on your Little League team, or did it take a while for your talent to develop?

Ryan, 8

Lessons of life

A I wasn't the best when I started because I was just learning, and I usually played with older, more experienced players. As time went on, I did become one of the key players on my team.

One lesson I learned early—and still believe today—is: No matter how good you are, you will find or meet someone who can—and will—outplay you on any given day. That lesson has always helped me keep my head on straight.

Q What were you like as a child?

Melissa

Lasting qualities

A Besides growing up kind of skinny and gangly and, at times, uncoordinated, I recall the following traits about myself:
- I was always athletic and loved taking part in sports.
- I respected my elders, my mother, etc., and I remember feeling awful on the few occasions that I did anything that disappointed or angered her.
- I had an ability to draw, but I never fully developed that skill.
- I liked adventure, challenge and travel.
- Going way back, I always thought I had a talent for making people laugh.

Most of these traits I still have today, though you won't always see them when I'm interviewed or on the playing field.

Q Were there obstacles you had to overcome to reach your goal of becoming a professional baseball player?

Lisa, 12

Everyone faces obstacles

My Life

A Everyone who has a goal in life faces obstacles. The key is how to overcome them.

Some of the obstacles for me were: dealing with the short playing seasons in Minnesota; achieving the level at which I wanted to play, because I had no successful role model; suffering a couple of injuries; and adjusting to a new position when I was switched from pitching to the outfield.

I also had to learn the techniques and skills to enable me to succeed against tough college competition around the country.

Finally, I had to deal with peers who tried to deter me from my goal. I put on blinders to distractions and did whatever was necessary to be successful in my field, and you can, too.

Happy with life

Q If you could start life over, would you live it the same, or what would you change?
Anna, 12

A Even after all these years, I can say that, other than a few regrets—and maybe wishing I knew one or two times what was in people's hearts or what their true motives were at key times—I honestly wouldn't change many things.

I really don't wish to be anyone else. I'm not jealous of others. I'm glad to have the family and friends I have, and I would not wish to grow up in a different era. Satisfied may not be the word to describe my life, but then again, there's not much I would change. I just say my prayers of thanks every day.

Sandlot successes

Q Has anybody else from St. Paul's old Oxford Playground ever made a career out of baseball or any other sport?
Anonymous

Childhood Memories

A There were some extremely talented athletes who played or practiced there over the years. I don't know about them playing in the professional ranks, but I know a couple of guys who had stellar college careers.

In addition to Toronto Blue Jay Paul Molitor, who played or practiced there occasionally, there was LeRoy Gardner, a star basketball player at the University of Minnesota. And Gopher basketball greats Lou Hudson and Archie Clark played some pickup games and basketball games there in the summer, although they're not from Minnesota.

I think Oxford was known over the years as much for its coaches and coaching as for its players.

SANDLOT START: The Blue Jays' Paul Molitor is among other athletic stars to emerge from St. Paul.

PIONEER PRESS FILE PHOTO

Q When you were playing American Legion ball for Attucks Brooks, do you remember the monstrous home run you hit at Harding High School in St. Paul to win the game 3-0?
Nick

Early success

A It's been so long since I played there that I can't recall all the games or incidents of my formative years. But since coming to the Minnesota Twins, I've already heard from many people who played with or against me while I was growing up here in St. Paul.

Q Did you collect baseball cards as a kid, and do you collect them now?
Ed

Different era

A Actually, I collected marbles. I purchased unique marbles and won countless others in the games we'd play with friends. The few baseball cards I acquired were used for a different purpose than kids do today. I put them in the spokes of my bike as noisemakers.

The old neighborhood

Q **Where did you live as a kid in St. Paul, and do you ever go back to that neighborhood?**
Jacob, 10

A I lived at two different addresses on Carroll Avenue, less than one block from the playground that is now called Jimmy Lee Recreation Center. I still visit the area frequently to see relatives and friends.

No regrets

Q **What was your childhood like growing up in St. Paul? Any regrets?**
David

A Growing up in a single-parent family, we didn't have much money, many clothes or material things—no family car, no summer cabin or even magazine subscriptions.

But what we did have were good role models in the family. We had neighbors and families in the community where we could spend time in their homes. Very importantly, all of our friends were of different colors and backgrounds, and we all played together. Looking back, I don't think I'd trade too much with the kids of today.

No limits

Q **Did growing up black limit your chances to participate in activities with other kids?**
Andy, 13

A Being raised in St. Paul in the '50s and '60s, I fortunately had no problems with race that prevented me from participating in activities with other kids. It's really shameful when a person or

Childhood Memories

organization prevents innocent kids from participating in activities because of race or color.

Q: Do you miss your Central High days in St. Paul?

Zeke, 18

A: Not as much as some people might think. I feel my life has continued to get more exciting and enriching. My days at Central were fun, and I can look back fondly on them. No doubt I developed much of my character and capabilities from friends, teachers and others I worked with back then.

Life exciting then and now

WINFIELD FOUNDATION

TEAM EFFORTS: Dave and his high-school teammates.

Chapter 2

DAVE DATA:
In 1982, Dave hits a career-high 37 home runs, becoming only the ninth player to hit 30 or more home runs in both the American and National Leagues.

STEPHEN WUNROW

CLASS MOVES: As a strong advocate for self-esteem programs and educational opportunities, Dave tries often to visit with kids in the classroom.

VITAL Stats

Quick start

Q Why didn't you play minor-league ball?
Max, 6

A Because I was drafted out of the University of Minnesota in three sports, I told the San Diego Padres that if I chose to play baseball, I must play immediately in the big leagues. After my first year of play, I earned my way into the starting lineup, and I haven't looked back since.

Love at first bat

Q Why did you decide to pursue a career in baseball?
Tom

Q What's kept you going all these years in baseball?
Mark

A You know how when you are young and see adults in an occupation and say, "I want to do that"? Well, that was me when I saw professional baseball players when I was 8 or 9 years old. And oh, how convenient it was for me to practice and play just a half-block from my house—and to have my brother, Steve, in the upper bunk to talk to about playing baseball every day and every night.

What keeps me going even today is my ability to perform at a high level and consistently still have

My Life

fun at work, and I still enjoy the many public and personal rewards for playing America's No. 1 pastime.

Off-season busy, too

Q: What do you do in the off-season?
Tony

A: Every year, I have a very busy off-season mixed with business, pleasure and training. Every professional athlete uses his time off quite differently.

In a typical off-season, I will manage my business affairs and investments, make personal appearances, speak at dinners, negotiate a new contract (if it's time), take a cruise or exotic trip and work out at a health club to prepare for the next baseball season.

I learned a long time ago to take some time out to stop and smell the roses, so to speak. If you work hard, you've got to take time to relax, too.

Retirement plans

Q: With your leadership skills, do you think you'll ever be interested in coaching or managing in the major leagues?
Joe, 18

A: I can't say that I have any plans to become a manager or coach. Although I understand the fundamentals and art of the game and how to motivate players to do their best, I don't think that I would want to be away from home and traveling almost nine months a year planning my strategies for my 40-man roster, coaching staff and the 162-game season.

Season's long grind

Q: What's the hardest part about being in the major leagues?
Michael, 15

Vital Stats

A Without a doubt, it's having to perform well while facing the best baseball players in the world every day for six months straight—and knowing that every newspaper, TV and radio station is reporting the results.

The other hard part is trying to stay healthy, strong and consistently productive all season long.

Q What do you do in your spare time?
Kelly, 9

Busy days and nights

A During the season, it seems, the days and games blend right into each other. Consequently, I spend most of my time resting and thinking about how I played the last game and then mentally preparing for the game to be played the next day. But like other people, I'll pay bills and stay on top of personal business. Sometimes, I'll have lunch at new and different restaurants, and when there are day games, maybe even take in an evening movie. On a recent off day, I went fishing with some of my teammates.

Q Why did you choose to play pro baseball over basketball?
Bjorn, 7

Baseball my first love

A I first started playing organized basketball as a senior in high school, but I started playing baseball at age 8. That's what led to my love of baseball.

It's only in the last 10 years or so that basketball has become the glamour sport that's attracted more

WINFIELD FOUNDATION

A college basketball star, too, Dave still enjoys an occasional game on the court.

My Life

and more kids. It was nowhere as hot as it is today when I was growing up.

Baseball lessons

Q What's the most important thing you've learned in your baseball career?
Ryan, 13

A Better yet, I'll give you the three most important things I've learned:
- The importance of teamwork.
- How to build relationships with different kinds of people.
- The benefits of testing and challenging my strength and capabilities every day.

School visits fun

Q How do you like visiting schools?
Pat, 14

A It's one of the things I've done many times during my career. It gives me a good chance to talk to and—just as important—listen to kids.

I believe I was one of the first ballplayers to start going to schools to discuss substance abuse. Beginning in 1989, my foundation developed a kit called "Turn It Around" with substance-abuse prevention material for elementary school children.

I receive many more invitations to schools than I could possibly accept. That's why I'm on videotape, so that I can participate when I cannot make personal appearances.

PHOTO COURTESY OF DAVE AND TONYA WINFIELD

GRADUATION DAY: Dave, who graduated from high school in 1969, helps others get a good education through the work of his Winfield Foundation.

Vital Stats

I'm very flattered that other baseball players, such as St. Louis Cardinals pitcher Bob Tewksbury, have asked me to help them design programs for their school visits.

Life in the Twin Cities

Q How does your wife like living in the Twin Cities, compared with the other cities where you've been?

Erica, 13

A Tonya says she likes it very much and has no problems here. When she told me that the Twin Cities even remind her a little bit of her home in New Orleans, I said, "How so?"

She says the people here are friendly, very warm and not so uptight. She's found that there are many different people and cultures in the cities here, it's easy to get around and there's always a lot of activity going on.

Balancing personal life and baseball

Q Do you ever feel you don't have enough time for family and personal matters because of baseball?

Katie, 11

WINFIELD FOUNDATION

FAMILY TIME: Dave and wife Tonya share reading time with daughter Shanel.

My Life

A With our schedule, it's always hard, but I wouldn't call it a problem. I find that it's very important to be disciplined and to plan my personal and business matters accordingly around baseball. In those rare instances of family emergencies, club management usually understands that the family comes first.

Big shoes to fill

Q What size shoe do you wear?

Anonymous

A I have a company that makes special-cut shoes for me. They're size 13 1/2 with an E width. A big man needs a good foundation!

WINFIELD FOUNDATION

TALL ORDER: At a towering 6 foot 6, Dave really has to search to find a taller compatriot.

Vital Stats

Q: What size bat do you use, and how many bats do you go through in a year?
— Sharon, 8

Big bats, big hits

A: I use a bat that is 35½ inches long and, most of the time, 33 ounces. That has been pretty standard for me for the last 10 years. Including spring training, batting practice and regular games during the season, I break about 60 bats per year.

Q: How often do you read for pleasure? What kind of materials do you enjoy reading? What do you feel the importance of reading is, and do you think it is necessary to be able to read well to be a successful athlete? When do you find time to read?
— Dustin

Reading for pleasure

A: I read something every day. I start with the newspapers. Then would come newsletters, magazines or books. It's essential to know what's happening in the world and in the state and city where you live to know how your life will be affected.

I subscribe to newsletters for financial information and to magazines for trends, styles and what's happening with people. In books, I'm drawn more toward fact than fiction. I like biographies, self-improvement and intrigue. I'll read at home or on the road—it doesn't matter.

Now an athlete doesn't have to be a good reader to be successful, but quite a few successful athletes will tell you that they've gained instruction, philosophy, techniques and wisdom from other people through books, and not just in person from a coach.

My Life

No pets allowed

Q: Do you have any pets?
Anonymous, 8

A: No. My job in baseball, with all the travel during the season and my business concerns off-season, has never allowed me to have a pet. However, if I could, I would first have a very large aquarium with lots of tropical fish. Then I'd choose a dog, possibly a Dalmatian—or a bulldog, so I could smile at its sagging face each day.

Keeping in touch

Q: Why did you start Ask Dave?
Anonymous

A: First, it was because I received so much mail from kids and adults alike from around the country—and now in Minnesota—asking many of the same questions. I thought this would be a great way for me to respond to them.

Second, I did a similar kind of thing with my own radio show when I played with the California Angels. It was called "On the Ball . . . With Dave Winfield."

Best friends

Q: Who's your best friend in baseball?
Nate 10

Q: Who were some of your favorite teammates before coming to Minnesota?
Steve, 11

A: I really don't have one clear-cut best friend because I never played in the minor leagues with some of the guys—and because there have been so many seasons with so many changes of employment and location.

But guys I'd list very high are Devon White, Joe Carter, Kirby Puckett, Dave Parker and one guy

Vital Stats

who was in my wedding—Don Baylor, the manager of the Colorado Rockies.

Q: Do you have any hobbies?
Chase, 9

A: Once a baseball season starts, I don't have much time to dabble in what I would call hobbies. But one activity I enjoy and would say comes closest to a hobby is photography. Since age 20, when I bought my first 35mm camera, I have enjoyed capturing images and special moments on film.

Photography longtime favorite activity

Chapter 3

DAVE DATA:
In 1984, Dave has a career-high 20-game hitting streak, wins his fifth Gold Glove and finishes second to Yankee teammate Don Mattingly with a career-high .340 batting average.

ASSOCIATED PRESS

MEDIA FOCUS: Signing with the New York Yankees in 1980, Dave spent a tumultuous decade in the Big Apple and the city's bright spotlight.

THE SPOTLIGHT'S Glare

Q: What's it like to be well-known and world-famous?
— Monica, 10

A: To be well-known and world-famous is like a coin—it has two sides. There is the good, and there is the bad.

The two sides of fame

CHRIS POLYDOROFF/ST. PAUL PIONEER PRESS

VIEWER FRIENDLY: Dave is at ease on the baseball field or in front of a TV camera.

My Life

On the good side, it's a lot of fun, with many people wanting to do many things for you. You get to meet famous people, visit faraway places and have many adventures. The fame can attract many good things to you.

But on the flip side, it can bring out jealousy, greed and dislike in people and cause a loss of privacy. You can't go to restaurants or the malls. As Michael Jordan found in Atlantic City in 1993, you may not be left alone. If you have a personal problem or make a mistake in judgment, millions of people know about it that very day.

Always in the spotlight

Q **As a role model for many youngsters, how much pressure do you feel not to screw up?**
Michael, 12

NO ESCAPE: Michael Jordan is one of many star athletes whose every action is monitored by the media and the public.

ASSOCIATED PRESS

A The role-model discussion is a big one today, as is clear from the Charles Barkley and Michael Jordan headlines in 1993. I learned, while in college and early as a young professional, that I did influence youngsters and could do so in a positive way.

Fortunately, the values I learned while growing up enable me to just be myself, not to change a whole lot to please others or worry a lot about how others perceive me.

Dealing with defeat

Q **How would you have dealt with the situation if the Blue Jays had lost the World Series in 1992?**
Daniel, 12

The Spotlight's Glare

A I can only guess about my answer here. On the one hand, after a down period if we had lost, I might have decided to return to the Blue Jays for the one-year opportunity that was offered and try to win it again with the same nucleus.

Generally speaking, though, after a team loses a heartbreaking World Series that is highly publicized—as we did with the Yankees in 1981—most players try to get away from the baseball fans and media opinions. Many take their families on vacation and try not to take the loss too personally.

I've found that it's best not to keep the negative thoughts or feelings within yourself too long. After the 1981 World Series, I made sure that I got involved in other positive activities within two weeks.

Q Do you ever get nervous at the plate, and, if so, how do you handle it?

Reid, 9

Pressure to perform

A Sure I get nervous! Every player who cares about doing his best gets anxious or has butterflies, particularly in critical game situations. You also want to succeed for yourself, your team and the millions of fans watching the game in the stadium and on TV.

You try to combat that nervousness with a positive attitude, knowledge and images of previous successes in similar situations.

Remember, too, that even the best hitters in baseball—those with .300 averages—fail seven out of 10 times at bat. You have to have high self-esteem and believe in yourself to be a successful athlete.

Q What's it feel like always being asked for your autograph?

Anonymous

Autograph seekers

My Life

Q How do you feel about signing autographs?

A Most of the time, it feels good, but just so you know: It's not possible for me to give an autograph any time or any place that people ask me for one. A bad time, for example, is when I'm on the field minutes before competition or while I'm at dinner with my family—I've even been asked for my autograph in the restroom.

Otherwise, I try to sign at least a few autographs in public each day, as well as returning a few by mail.

Disappointing some fans inevitable

Q How do you feel about signing autographs for older fans? We're not collectors—just fans—and we were disappointed when you passed us by.

Eric, 19, and Marty, 17

A Hey, guys, I hope you understand that every day when I arrive at the ballpark, leave the stadium or walk the streets, there is always someone who goes away disappointed because I'm not able to honor every autograph request.

For the few that I am able to sign, I try to find the youngest fan with that gleam in his eyes or people that I know don't make a habit of seeking these autographs. In those few moments, inevitably I'm going to overlook someone. Perhaps we'll meet again at the right time and I'll be able to accommodate you.

Handling the obnoxious few

Q How do you handle really obnoxious fans?
Mike, 12

Q Have you ever been really mad at a heckler?
Paul, 9

A Obnoxious fans sometimes make it rough on us athletes—and distracting for the diehard fans trying to watch the game, as well.

84

Most athletes tend to hear those occasional loudmouths with bad things to say more than they hear the good things other fans say. Most of us try to have a thick skin, overlook the real bozos and stay focused.

In terms of hecklers, yes, I've gotten mad and responded to them before. I've had a couple of perfect comebacks where I've silenced a heckler by slamming a home run and then wagging my finger at them as I've crossed home plate. Also, if a heckler gets on me before a game starts, I have confronted him in a crowd with some good lines that I have that usually embarrass and silence those kind of people.

Chapter 4

DAVE DATA:
Dave began the Winfield Foundation in 1977 primarily to provide scholarships and help underprivileged kids. It since has branched out into highly regarded self-esteem and drug-prevention programs.

ASSOCIATED PRESS

WEIGHING IN: Dave lends his stature as a superstar to causes promoting health and education programs for the young.

YOUTH
Efforts

Q: What gave you the idea to start the Dave Winfield Foundation?
Katie, 11

A: My basic feelings about helping others absolutely came from my family influences and values—and from the area in which I grew up.

Family values

WINFIELD FOUNDATION

SECRET IDENTITY? Size-wise, he'll never be mistaken for a Jolly Old Elf, but Dave does fill-in duty for Santa at a community Christmastime dinner.

My Life

My mother always thought about and cared about others. She contributed in many ways on behalf of the less fortunate.

I also believe that being from Minnesota helped shape my feelings and beliefs. Minnesota is a national leader when it comes to giving.

When I turned professional, one of the first things I thought about was how I could give back to the community in thanks for the many people who helped me succeed.

Foundation efforts going strong

Q **How are your programs for youths faring these days?**

David

CITY SALUTE: Dave joins St. Paul Mayor Jim Scheibel to congratulate kids who participated in his 1993 urban Rookie League baseball program.

GINGER PINSON/ST. PAUL PIONEER PRESS

A The Winfield Foundation, the organization I created in 1977, continues to provide programs to youths across the country and is still going strong.

In Minnesota, I'm able to focus on a couple of efforts—one is the Newspaper in Education program through the Saint Paul Pioneer Press, which will take up some of my time. The other is a local scholarship program that has my name on it. That program is in its 18th year.

Like most civic-minded athletes of today, my fellow players and I do what we can without spreading ourselves too thin. But over the years, I've learned that we spend a lot of time at the stadium and/or preparing for that work during the season, so it limits our involvement.

Anyone wanting more information about the Winfield Foundation can write in care of:

The Winfield Foundation
One Bridge Plaza
Suite 400
Fort Lee, N.J. 07024

Q Why did you make the "Turn It Around" video?
Angela, 8

A Since 1977, when I created a nonprofit foundation, our goal has been to provide health and educational opportunities through my platform in sports.

After creating and supporting many programs over the years, we decided to turn our attention and resources to the battle against drugs. Using prevention techniques on youths in elementary schools was key to us.

After speaking to thousands of kids at many

Video helps spread anti-drug message

My Life

schools, I felt it was necessary to duplicate our message through the use of a videotape, a poster and a lesson plan that teachers and youth workers could share with their groups.

I'm happy we went this route, because the "Turn It Around" program has been an unqualified success in many areas across the country.

Q What advice do you give children regarding the importance of school?

Kathleen, fourth-grade teacher

A Since most adults' message to kids about education is simply "Stay in school," or "Get an education," or "Hit the books because it's important," many times it goes in one ear and out the other. I tell kids this about education:

Education is knowledge, information about everything and how things are related to each other. Education is a lifelong experience. Learn something every day of your life—everywhere—not just when you're young and sitting in the classroom.

The more you know about things, the more opportunities you will have for a good life that you are in control of. The less you know, the more limited your choices in life are, and you will be sure to get the bottom of the barrel on anything important.

So, read every day. Travel and meet people, and you will broaden your horizons. Once your mind is open and expanded to new possibilities and options, it will never go back to its original size.

Q Are you involved in the anti-drug effort DARE, and what do you think of the program?

Neil, 12

Youth Efforts

A For the past six or seven years, through my foundation, we have addressed the substance-abuse problem from a prevention standpoint. We call our program "Turn It Around," and we focus on self-esteem, goals, choices, positive alternatives and trust. This is where we felt we could make the most impact with young kids.

Early on, during the course of my information-gathering, I found that one of the high-quality elementary-school programs that was accepted and used across the United States was DARE. I applaud the program, the police and their efforts, and the schools that adopt this program. It's top-notch.

Chapter 5

DAVE DATA:
In 1990, after missing the entire 1989 season, Dave is traded to the California Angels, gets his 2,500th hit and is named Comeback Player of the Year.

ASSOCIATED PRESS

IN THE SWING: Dave loosens up before entering the batter's box as part of his familiar warm-up routine.

KEEPING FIT

Q: What do you eat, and what kinds of exercises do you do during the season to be able to play up to your expectations?
— Josh, 14

A: I learned a long time ago from books, advice and real-life experiences that what I eat is the fuel for my body and my performance. Now, I eat much more chicken, fish and seafood than I do beef, and I've tried to eliminate pork from my diet.

I also eat a wide variety of fruits and vegetables. Vitamins and mineral supplements are important, too, because of the hard, stressful work I do.

Off season, after my rest period, I usually go to the health club four to five days a week to spend an hour and a half working out with weights, doing cardiovascular exercises and maybe a little basketball.

In season, I do less weight work but a lot of stretching exercises. My focus is maintaining my strength while I play.

Such a schedule may seem like hard work or a hassle, but it's a lifestyle I've learned to like. You'll find that you will look and feel better at any age if you follow a routine of proper nutrition and exercise.

Diet and exercise are keys to fitness

Baseball season offers vigorous workout

THE BIG STRETCH: Dave preaches the value of warm-up exercises to prevent injuries and perform at peak levels.

ASSOCIATED PRESS

Today's rehab programs can work wonders

Q **What exercises do you do to stay in shape?**
Sean, St. Anthony

A For me and others on the Twins, a steady diet of running, stretching, lifting weights, throwing and chasing balls and swinging the bat each day does the trick for us. But for any of you youngsters, I advise finding any sport or activity that gets your muscles flexed, your legs moving and helps you break a sweat at least three days a week. It's a great lifestyle to develop and gets you out from in front of the TV with your Nintendo or Sega Genesis games.

Q **What conditioning and training did you undergo after having back surgery to get back in playing condition? Are there things you can't do now as a result of your back problem?**
Joe

A The first two weeks or so after surgery, I did virtually nothing and took the time to heal. Over the next five months, I was on a pretty strict therapy and rehabilitation program using weights and a large green ball for my back exercises. I was supervised through countless repetitions of exercises to strengthen the stomach and back.

After missing an entire season—but by taking the time to repair myself—I was as close to good as new as I could get.

Keeping Fit

Fortunately, with modern medicine and surgery, today's doctors are able to correct problems that 50 years ago would have cut a career or active life short.

Q: What are some good warm-up exercises my softball team and I can do?
Allison, 12

A: First, I suggest you and your teammates do some jogging for up to five minutes to work up your core body temperature and break a sweat. Next, I would recommend stretching for five to 10 minutes. Concentrate on your hamstring muscles, back, legs and shoulders. You even might work in some jumping jacks.

Exercises and stretching are a must for any athlete. Many people do not know that most injuries are caused not principally by game situations, but by not warming up well enough beforehand.

Warm-up exercises are essential

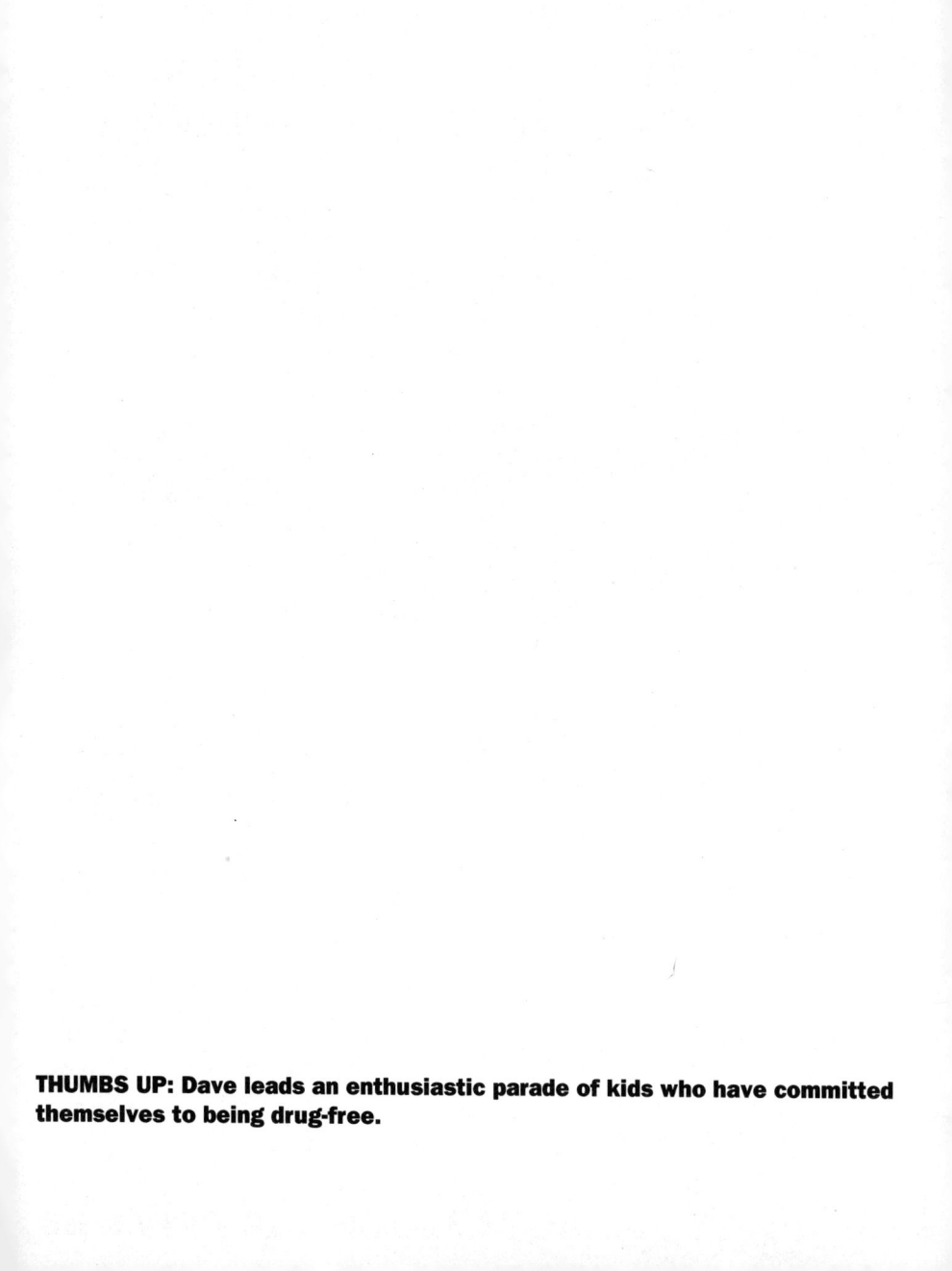

THUMBS UP: Dave leads an enthusiastic parade of kids who have committed themselves to being drug-free.

LEADING
The Way

WINFIELD FOUNDATION

WINFIELD FOUNDATION

CAREER AT A GLANCE

- Dave was born Oct. 3, 1951, in St. Paul, Minn., where he attended high school and played baseball, football and basketball.

  Vital Stats:
  Height: 6 foot 6
  Weight: 245
  Bats and throws right-handed

- He majored in political science and Afro-American studies at the University of Minnesota. At the University, he played basketball and baseball for the Minnesota Gophers. He served as team captain his senior year, going 13-1 as a pitcher while batting over .400. He holds the Gophers' single-season pitching record for strikeouts (109) and was selected to the All-America first team and was named Most Valuable Player of the 1973 College World Series.

- In 1973, he was drafted in three professional sports: baseball (San Diego Padres), football (Minnesota Vikings) and basketball (both the Utah Stars of the ABA and the Atlanta Hawks of the NBA).

- In 1977, he founded the David M. Winfield Foundation to help underprivileged children.

Vital Statistics

Leading the Way

• Over the years, he has won several major awards, including the YMCA Brian Piccolo Award for Humanitarian Services in 1979, the first Branch Rickey Community Service Award, the 1992 Arete Award for courage in sports and the American League's 1993 Joe Cronin Award for significant achievement. He also has received an honorary doctorate of laws from Syracuse University.

Baseball Milestones

• On Sept. 16, Dave became the 19th member of baseball's 3,000 Hit Club, singling off Oakland A's pitcher Dennis Eckersley.

• Through the 1993 season, Dave has 3,014 hits for a career batting average of .285. He has played in 2,850 games and has 453 home runs, including 11 grand slams; 1,786 RBIs; 1,058 extra-base hits; and 220 stolen bases.

• He is one of only eight players with 400 home runs and at least 2,800 hits, joining Hank Aaron, Babe Ruth, Willie Mays, Stan Musial, Mel Ott, Frank Robinson and Carl Yaztrzemski, all members of the Hall of Fame.

• Dave is the oldest player ever to drive in 100 runs in a season, accomplishing the feat in 1992 at age 41. In 1991, he became the oldest player ever to hit for the cycle and had the first three-homer game of his career.

• In 1990, he was named the American League's Comeback Player of the Year after missing the entire 1989 season with a back injury.

• Dave has won seven Gold Gloves and been named to 12 All-Star teams, seven times as a starter.

▲100▲

Leading the Way

The Winfield Foundation

"The only thing as powerful as his line drive is his commitment to our nation's youth. Dave Winfield's involvement with the community is an extension of his family life, education, athletic style and determination."

That statement from the David M. Winfield Foundation sums up the importance Dave places on helping the next generation get off to a good start.

"A lot of people don't know this, but he was the first active athlete to create a foundation," says Mario Casciano, foundation administrator. "His philosophy in life is that what you get out of it depends on what you put in."

Steve Winfield, Dave's brother and vice president of the foundation, agrees, stressing the family's upbringing as spurring their involvement: "Maybe because of the kind of giving, sharing person our mother was, it probably couldn't help but rub off on us. Not only our mother raising us, but our grandmothers and the cousins and the aunts, the volunteer coaches, the mentors and the fathers."

KID POWER: Dave joins kids in the community at the launch of his well-received "Turn It Around" self-esteem program.

Leading the Way

When the Winfield Foundation was created in 1977, it concentrated primarily on scholarships and other financial efforts to help underprivileged youths. But over the years, it has expanded its focus to deal with the wide range of threats to our nation's young people.

Today, its efforts still include scholarship programs but also encompass literacy efforts, health fairs and clinics, nutrition programs, community outreach, holiday celebrations, sports and fitness programs and a nationally acclaimed drug-prevention program.

That program, "Turn It Around," was begun in 1985 in cooperation with the Drug Enforcement Administration to focus on the self-esteem and decision-making issues often involved in substance abuse. The effort, endorsed by numerous education leaders and government agencies, originally aimed at high-school students. But as the decision to use drugs has been made at increasingly younger ages, the program has broadened its scope to reach kids as early as third grade.

For more information on the Winfield Foundation and the "Turn It Around" program, contact:

The David M. Winfield Foundation
One Bridge Plaza, Suite 400
Fort Lee, N.J. 07024
Phone: (201) 592-5031

HOW TO ORDER
Winfield Books

This commemorative book, following Dave Winfield's career from childhood through his 3000th hit, is available for $9.95, plus postage and handling.

This question-and-answer book, giving Dave Winfield's answers to kids' questions, is available for $7.95, plus postage and handling.

Call (800) 642-6480 to order.